Don't Be Stupid about Investing

DontBeStupid.club Answers to
Stocks, Bonds, Mutual Funds,
Real Estate and Retirement

H. Granville James

ITSUS
PRESS

Don't Be Stupid about Investing
DontBeStupid.club Answers to Stocks, Bonds, Mutual Funds,
Real Estate and Retirement

Legal Disclaimer: Everything in this book is the opinion of
the author. No responsibility is taken for the application or
use of these thoughts in any specific circumstances. The
reader should *Think for Yourself*.

ISBN: 1530795281
ISBN-13: 978-1530795284

Dedication

The DontBeStupid.club books about money are dedicated to John Bogle.

Mr. Bogle is not stupid about money.

"Saint Jack" stood virtually alone in the wilderness for decades. First millions of dollars, then billions and now trillions of dollars follow his ideas. His ideas, yes. His ideals? Not so much.

"Saint Jack" was not meant as a compliment originally. Legend says it started as an insult.

Among the ideals, there is a simple thesis that investors have no reason to pay high fees to expensive money managers. Investors will do better by paying lower fees for simpler products. It's a well-supported argument using critical thinking at a level we aspire to attain. But it really annoys people whose paychecks depend on fees.

"Saint Jack" is the founder of The Vanguard Group. He is single-handedly responsible for changing an industry, and for saving investors many billions of dollars in fees and expenses. It might even be a trillion by now. The whole industry has lower fees because they have to compete with "Saint Jack". We guess that makes stupid people resort to name calling.

Perhaps our favorite Bogle moment is from an interview on one of those financial shows. We paraphrase here;

Interviewer: You could make a lot more money.
Bogle: How much better would I eat?

Thank you, Saint Jack. Long may you run.

Contents

1.
Let's Begin

EVERYBODY WANTS TO be an investor. It sounds like something good to be. Being an investor gives us this warm feeling of our money doing all the work for us. We just kick back and relax, let our money work while we drink margaritas on the beach. Investing just "feels" that way when you say it, doesn't it? Being an investor means you're substantial. You're smart. You're special. And investing makes you rich!

Everyone wants to be an investor. Until they make a bad investment. My Investment lost money? How can this be? Isn't that wrong?

Yes, it is wrong. And much too frequently, it's also stupid. This book will stop the stupid part. We cannot guaranty all investments will make money, in fact most investments don't. But we can guarantee against stupidity if you follow our principles.

Stupid investments are always due to the lack of critical thinking (see DontBeStupid.club for a detailed look at all of our critical thinking principles; in this book, the principles used will be in *italics* to identify them). Stupid investments are made based on emotion and hope, not critical thinking. Sometimes you even get lucky and win. You know how the saying goes, even blind squirrels find acorns occasionally. True, but most of the time they die. And most of the time stupid investors lose.

The perception of investing as something noble is conditioned into us by a relentless stream of sales messages that start before we're born. We are programmed to have an emotional reaction and spend money. There are babies feeling tension right now because Mom is worrying about investing for their college education. She wasn't worried about it until someone selling 529 plans made her think about it. And now she's going to think about it until all the kids graduate. Because if she can't pay for it, then she's a failure, of course.

Investments are sold based on emotions. Once they get you thinking about investing, that money sucking sound doesn't end until you die. And hopefully you die before your investments run out, because death is better than living without investments. There are plenty of people out there, collecting fees of course, that will help you figure out "your number". You can't stop working until you have it. And then you have to keep it invested just right, because you can't live longer than your investments. Life without a portfolio is just not worth living.

Wait a minute... Do I even want to know my number? Actually, no. I don't. More on that later.

Fleecing, I mean "servicing", investors is a big business. Really big. There is a whole industry devoted to making you think you need their products and you need their help. Because you're behind! They should know because they set the target. So you have to invest more to catch up. Doesn't something feel wrong when these "helpers" have so much money, make ridiculous salaries and profits, while their customers are all behind? *Trust Common Sense.* Of course it's wrong. Don't be stupid. That's how they got rich.

We will cut through all of that bullshit for you. We promise to *Simplify,* as we always do, and you will understand investing at a level better than most professionals charging for their advice. The goal is for you to confidently manage your own money, listen to others when you think it's worth your time, and evaluate investment opportunities from a position of knowledge rather than emotion. It's not as complicated as everyone tries to make it.

Don't Be Distracted. Resolve right now to never invest in something because it "sounds good" or it's a "hot" time for it, or only your brother-in-law has the secret info. Resolve to do the analysis and invest only based on answers reached through critical thinking. Use the principles in this book. Make this commitment to your investments and you will be ahead of the average investor before even finishing this first chapter.

At the end of this book, we'll give you a couple of easy investing answers that have seen plenty of our hard-core analysis. And the truth is, those easy answers are good enough for everyone who does not want to get seriously into this investing game.

If you want to put in the time and effort, then yes, you can be almost as good as the professional sharks. You have to enjoy it enough, be fascinated by numbers and human nature and other ethereal interactions. Some days we get in the mood for all that and it becomes fun. Most people have better things to do with their time, and we've done the work already anyway, so our easy answers are included at the end.

But we want to make sure you understand investing first. That's why easy answers are at the END. Even if you don't want to put much energy into investing, it's important you understand it well enough so you don't fall for some sales pitch or other "hot tip" along the way. The sales pressure is everywhere. You need a real understanding to deflect it. Our goal is for you to recognize the bullshit when it hits you, even if you don't plan to do much hard-core investment analysis for yourself.

First Things First. The chapters in this book are in order. Follow the order. Each chapter requires understanding the one prior. If something later on sounds more interesting, don't skip ahead. If you're interested in a Commodity but haven't read the Stock chapter yet, just stay awake an extra hour and read it all. Then read it again tomorrow, because you were probably half asleep at the end anyway…

And we assume everyone has read "Don't Be Stupid about Money". If not, *First Things First.* Read our first book about money. If you don't think about money the way we do, then our discussions on investing are premature. Plus, we poked fun at "bears" and "corrections" and some other "sacred cows" in the Money book, so we can't just repeat those observations here. But we enjoyed that and want to know you've read them too.

This book is a little more challenging than most we write. It assumes you really want to understand investing. If you cannot tolerate a little dry reading to actually understand investing, then you should not buy this book. And you also should not invest, because that's how stupid people lose money.

This book is about understanding investing. It is not another "do this, do that, and you will be rich" book. We hope you finish this book understanding investing enough to feel confident in any discussion. This book is not extremely heavy on math and calculations. We intend a real understanding of the guiding principles, and not so much hard-core analysis of specific investments.

Investing is a game. We play with real money. *Follow the Money.* All of the rules favor our opponents, because they make the rules. But investing is still a game you can win if you're not stupid. The opponents are actually very stupid, and they assume you are too. And that's how we win. We're just a little less stupid.

So let's all get a little less stupid about investing.

2.
What is Investing?

DEFINE THE TARGET. Investing – To put money into shares, property, commercial venture or financial schemes with the expectation of achieving a profit.

Note the word "scheme" in the definition is not intended to imply a negative commentary. The good people at the Oxford dictionary intend it to be used in the pure sense. A scheme is just a plan for putting an idea into effect. So, in this definition, it simply means a plan to make money. Unfortunately, our more sinister understanding of "scheme" accompanies investing way too often. But more on that later.

Anything we do with the expectation of getting back more value than we put in, that's investing. It's important to remember that clearly. Part of effective sales technique is to limit the prospect's choices. *Think for Yourself*. When you have money to invest, it's important not to let anyone else define investing for you.

ANYTHING you do with your money intending to make more money is investing.

Immediately this should open your mind to ideas outside traditional investment products. If you've seen or heard too many people advising the "right" balance of stocks and bonds for your age, you might start to believe those are your only choices. *Follow the Money.* People selling stocks and bonds would like you to forget you have other choices. Don't fall for this sales technique. Make your best choice from among all possibilities.

Very few people have enough money to buy every investment opportunity they encounter. And if they do, they will not have enough money for very long. Because here is a dirty little secret, most investments are stupid. Most of the time, the investor isn't as sexy as they think. Most investors are investing with their emotions. The people selling the investments are making the real profits.

We've all encountered more losers than winners. Losers are usually the ones bragging about a great investment they made. But they lose most of the time and just don't admit it. Or maybe they don't even know it. People are happy to talk about their success, and talk even more about their potential success, but their losses remain private. These people are stupid. They're emotionally involved. And emotions make stupid investments.

We have to choose the best investments for our money. To make choices that are not stupid, an evaluation without emotions must be done. We have an almost infinite universe of investments to choose from, but just a finite amount of money to invest. We have to choose from among all the clutter. We need decisions based on critical thinking.

Not only will well-reasoned decisions make better investments, there is an additional benefit that makes the world a better place. You will reduce the profits at companies cashing in on stupid investments.

Everyone jokes about buying swampland in Florida. But people do it every day. The "swamps" move around, but the tactics stay exactly the same. 1) Tell the prospect a uniquely interesting story, 2) Make the prospect feel special, and 3) Create an urgency to purchase. *Simplify.* Look for those three warning signs. If you see them, just say no. The vast majority of good investments do not have even one of those elements present in the evaluation. Two or three together just scream DON'T BE STUPID.

Here's a quick example. "I have three of this coin that was only minted in the year 2000 for the millennium. And we're really lucky to run into each other just now because I was about to put them up for auction on EBay. I need the money for a root canal because this back molar is just killing me. If you want to buy all three right now, I'll take half of what I'm going to ask on EBAY because this is so much faster and I'm really in pain. How about $50 per coin? Thanks for helping me out." You look at the coins and buy them. Isle of Man Crown coins from 2000 look really cool. And you can buy them for about $15 on Amazon or EBay.

That was a simple one, easily analyzed and defeated if you just ignore the emotions and take the time to do the analysis. But the method is practiced relentlessly. The world of investment choices gets more complicated, and the sales tactics more subtle and convincing. But *Don't Be Distracted.* You can cut through all the bullshit by doing the analysis without emotion. In the above case, all you had to do was Google the coin. But if someone is trying to sell you a variable annuity with downside protection, it's not so easy to see the flaws. (Don't ever buy one.)

Stupid Investing is a huge industry existing within the world of legitimate investing. Sometimes the stupid investment is even being sold by the same people selling good investments. And frequently the salesperson doesn't even know the difference. They can be very passionate about selling that variable annuity. *Think for Yourself.* We have to do our own analysis.

We use the words "Sold" and "Selling" next to "Investing" deliberately. We need to make the point strongly here. Investing is driven by salespeople chasing a paycheck. Do not ever be confused. Selling for profit is what drives the world of investing. That is not necessarily a bad thing, but it is no different than the salesperson selling you a car at the dealership. And usually adding the "true coat" to protect the paint job. Their paycheck depends on you buying. *Follow the Money.* Everyone wants you to buy something, and frequently they sell you what makes the most money for them, not what's best for you.

No one is more motivated than you to do the best possible evaluations for your own money. Keeping a clear understanding of what investing means, and avoiding stupid investments, is step one of any successful investing career. You cannot trust to blind luck in a universe saturated with salespeople. You have to evaluate and invest with a real, calculated expectation of getting more back out than you put in. This has to be a reliable expectation, critically analyzed and quantifiable. It cannot be hope or emotion.

The DontBeStupid.club Summary:

- Investing means putting money into something expecting to get a greater amount back out.
- We have to make investment choices based on critical thinking.

3.
Where Do I Start?

FIRST THINGS FIRST. At this point, we need a little review from our book "Don't Be Stupid about Money". "Investing" as it's traditionally thought of should not be terribly common. There are many better uses for our money, better Investments for our money, than stocks and bonds and real estate, etc. To be ready to invest means you have no fear of paying next month's expenses, and you have extra money looking to go to work. Most likely you have no debt either, because paying down any debt is a risk-free investment yielding a pretty decent return. Remember, every place we pay money to get more back in return is an investment.

OK, so now we are sure we're ready to buy some traditional investments. Let's get used to saying that right now, we "buy" investments. *Don't Be Distracted.* We don't "make investments". It's a name change that sounds like something better; "make" sounds like something nobler than "buy". But we don't make anything except the decision to buy something. The range of misleading terms for investing your money is truly astonishing. All of them exist for the sole purpose of distracting us. Always remember, wherever we bleed money, someone just hangs a bucket.

Simplify. Evaluate your alternatives, make the best choice and then buy. That's all there is to investing. It's almost too easy. But where do we start?

We start by knowing how to evaluate the purchase. And this is where most investors get stupid. Right at the start, they get stupid. They take the emotional journey created by someone else trying to sell something.

Don't Be Distracted. The story, the pictures, and your enormous future wealth from the investment are all very exciting. Brochures are compelling. They are well-crafted sales pitches, just like a new car brochure. Sales brochures masquerading as annual reports are more insidious and sometimes even more compelling. Look at the smiling faces in Microsoft's annual report... must be a good investment, right? Look at all the happy people. All of this is worth exactly zero in a real evaluation. Let's say it again, *Don't Be Distracted*.

How many times have you heard an investment evaluated as hot, rapid growth, aggressive, value oriented, safe, and so on... Do you notice that all of those words have a positive connotation? For example, why is "aggressive" not called "risky"? *Don't Be Distracted*. All adjectives and sales pitches are stupid reasons to make an investment. Starting today, they mean nothing to you. They are worth exactly zero in an investment evaluation.

To make an investment that's not stupid *There Will Be Math*. So let's learn to evaluate.

First Things First. We start with risk vs. return. More familiarly called risk vs. reward, if you like, but "return" is the more accurate term for an investment.

Rewards can include many intangibles. With an investment, the goal is a money profit.

Define the Target. Risk – Exposure to possible harm or loss.

Define the Target. Return – Profit from an investment.

Risk vs. Return is our possible harm compared to the expected profit from the investment.

Nothing can be done intelligently without understanding the risk vs. return of the potential investment. And it saves time if you do it first. *First Things First.* We can ignore anything that does not get past this initial analysis, all the stories and pretty pictures are just a waste of your time.

Simplify. Getting the risk vs. return analysis correct eliminates most of the clutter among our investment choices. We don't waste time on the emotions. The vast majority of available investments will not be correct for our risk and return profile. When you define your risk vs. return situation first, the list of good choices shrinks considerably. A shorter list makes the right answers easier to find and wastes less of your time.

With a clear understanding of risk and return, we are ready to proceed to the next step of getting started. We need to define our own personal starting point. We need to specify three things for ourselves.

1) What do we consider a risk-free return?

2) What return is my goal for the money to be invested?

3) How much greater risk am I willing to take on this investment?

And you must answer these for yourself. No one else can tell you your goals, or your tolerance for risk. Risk-free return is easier to define and outside input may help with that, but you have to put it all together for yourself.

An example of risk-free return: You invent a time machine and can return to 1997 to buy Amazon stock at the IPO. You know where the stock is going, so in this case, you have a risk-free return of around 37% annually.

Until we perfect that time machine, we'll need something more readily available today. So for our risk-free return, we will use a one-year CD at an FDIC-insured bank as our benchmark. It's about 1% right now as we write this. So if we have $10,000 to invest, then one year from today we will get back $10,100 guaranteed. That's our risk-free baseline. Anything with risk is going to have to pay off better than that or there is no incentive to take the risk.

Don't laugh off the time-machine example, though. For most people, looking around a little will identify some better risk-free returns available. How about if we travel into the future instead of the past? For example, can you get a 10% discount for paying your next year of rent in advance? (Try it. We've done it more than once.) That is a risk-free return of 10% on the money invested.

Your highest possible risk-free return is always the baseline in your analysis of any investment. Anything with risk has to return more profit. You take the risk-free return unless something offers enough incentive to accept the associated risks. Repeat that concept until it becomes automatic in your thinking. Paying rent in advance sounds boring, there is no sexy sales brochure. But when you understand you just scored a zero-risk after-tax return of 10% on your investment, that's not boring. Real profits are far more exciting than any sales brochure.

Ok, we have our risk-free return as a baseline and we understand the concept of comparing risk to return. Next?

What is our goal? What do we want this investment to accomplish? Let's say we have to pay junior's tuition a year from now, and if we don't, he's going to live in our future game room for another whole year. Seriously, identifying goals is the easiest part of the investing process. Yet people invest all the time just because they think something sounds like a good investment. That's stupid. Know your goals. In this case we want a pool room and junior must go.

Next, how much risk will we accept to meet our goal of getting junior out and our pool table in? *First Things First*. Maybe the answer is zero; no risk at all is the baseline. Is our risk-free return enough? If we have $10,000 to invest, our goal is getting on with junior's future ASAP, and the tuition payment is $10,100 dollars one year from now, then we will be highly motivated to choose our risk-free return of 1% on the CD. We know it's risk-free and we will have no problem making the payment when due. Junior is waving goodbye one year from now. Smart investment: goal met, zero risk, rack 'em up.

Needing only 1% return was great. But what if the payment due is $12,000? Our goal is now a 20% return. Risk-free is not going to get it done. We are now highly motivated to take more risk in the pursuit of the 20% return we need. Risk vs. Return. We want to make 20% but we cannot do it without accepting some risk. We are trying to make 20%, but we might make less or even lose money instead. But if we need 20% or else there is no pool table, then what choice do we have? We are highly motivated to accept whatever risk we must.

But maybe our investing goal is just that we want a new car. And if we fail, we just keep driving the old one. This feels less urgent to us. For this goal, we might take on a little risk, but we're not going to get too crazy about it. Maybe we'd be willing to accept a 10% chance of losing 30% in exchange for the 90% chance we'll make 20% profit? It depends on how much you want the new car, and how much you care about the risk of losing the investment money. Ultimately risk vs. return is a personal decision only you can make.

One good bet for chasing 20% over the next year is to buy some Amazon common stock. It's volatile enough up and down to spike 20%, and also tends to go up over longer periods of time. So it might get us a 20% return next year, and we probably won't lose the entire investment no matter what happens. This is definitely a more risky choice than our risk-free CD, but if we want 20% instead of 1% then we have to take some risk.

There really is no perfect answer for everyone, it depends on your goal for the investment return and your tolerance for possible harm in trying to get there.

Some people are gamblers by nature and will accept greater risk than others. In general, it helps to reconcile your goals with your nature. You cannot have a gambler's goals and expect to get there with low-risk investments. For example, we hate risk, so we avoid goals that chase 20% annual returns.

People have a way of judging investors after the results are in. Gamblers who win are sexy. And the ones who lose are just losers. *Think for Yourself*. That type of judgment is stupid. And the people judging this way are stupid. Set goals based on your priorities, and pursue those goals at whatever your comfort level with risk.

If you're a gambler, you've already considered the higher probability of losing. If you happen to lose, it doesn't come as a shock and you are prepared to absorb the loss. Winning or losing isn't what makes an investment decision good or bad. What makes it a good decision is knowing your risks and expecting a return that makes the risk worth taking.

Any investor who does not answer the basic questions correctly before proceeding? They're making bad decisions. You must know your risk-free return, your goal, and how much risk is attached to the higher return. These are easy questions that usually take only a few minutes to apply to every investment choice, once you're in the habit of doing it.

By the way, that 37% from the time machine, or the 1% on the CD, or the 20% profit on Amazon stock (if it goes up, like we hoped), those are our ROI. ROI means Return On Investment. The 1% interest paid on the CD is the "ROI" on that CD. Just divide the profit by the investment amount and the answer is ROI. It sounds more like you're a real investor when you speak in acronyms, so never say you made $2,000 profit on your $10,000 investment. Say your ROI was 20%. Much sexier.

So that's where we start. And that's all there is to know about where to start. Know your goals, and do the risk versus return evaluation for every single dollar you invest. Do this and now you are even farther ahead of most investors than when we started just a few paragraphs ago.

In most cases we observe, people take more risk than their goals demand, take more risk than necessary for the return they're getting, and are unable to connect the risk vs. return to their goals. Frequently people have not even defined their goal, they just think they should be "investing". And all of this is stupid.

In most cases, we see ways to get the same return or better in alternate choices with less risk. And that's not because we know something special, it's because we've done the analysis so we have something real to evaluate. There is no emotion, only critical thinking.

But our bigger concern is when we observe people accepting far too much risk for their circumstances. It's one thing to get 3% return when you should be getting 5% for the same level of risk. At least you still gain a little. But it's much more dangerous to see people taking 50% risks to chase 20% returns when what they really need is 5% to live on. In most cases, they do not understand the risk and are just hoping for the return.

This is really stupid and potentially painful investing.

Everyone understands the concept of risk vs. reward. Why do so few people actually get specific about it with their investments? Emotional investing. *Don't Be Distracted*. Doing the analysis eliminates the emotional stupidity. Frequently analysis yields an answer you don't want to hear. The right answers have no emotion attached. Sometimes the right answer just sucks. But you don't lose money with it.

Ok, we are committed to choosing among our investing options based on our goals and the associated risk vs. return analysis. Now what?

This is where we stop one last time and re-evaluate our risk-free return number. Remember, risk-free return is the profit we make on an investment that has ZERO RISK to our money. To take any risk at all, we have to expect a return higher than the risk-free return, otherwise why bother? If we can have a certain return for ZERO risk, then we will only consider a riskier choice if we expect higher returns.

All the time, and we mean ALL too frequently, you hear financial professionals refer to risk-free return as the return on a US Government security, usually the three-month T-Bill. And nothing could be more wrong for most people. Repeating an example we've already mentioned, if you have any debt, paying it off is risk-free return. For most people, their risk-free return value is equal to their most expensive debt, not a T-Bill. Paying down debt is 100% certain to yield the interest expense saved. That is risk-free return. If you have no debt at all, and no place else to look for risk-free return, then a three-month T-Bill becomes an acceptable measure.

Because it makes the discussion easier, let's just use 1% as our risk-free baseline. We actually like 1-year CD's more than 3-month T-Bills as a risk-free baseline anyway. The CD yields more and we can't find any difference in the risk. In fact, the US government risks shutting down more often than an FDIC insured bank. We'd argue the CD is actually safer in addition to yielding more.

In fact, let's use this as an example of making the best choice for an investing goal. If our goal is maximum return with zero risk, should anyone choose the T-Bill? The T-Bill yields only about half of our CD. Why would anyone choose to give up the difference? We don't know. We think the choice is obvious. The CD yields double with no additional risk. Every CD is not the same, but plenty of high quality banks offer them at double the yield of the 3-month T-Bill. Insured by the FDIC too. You have to spend a minute to do the analysis and then shop around. Maybe some people are too lazy. But being lazy with investments is stupid.

Once we've settled on our risk-free baseline, in this discussion we're using 1% annually, we're ready to evaluate choices where we expect better returns. Are you willing to accept the chance of losing 20% of your investment to make 50%? Most would answer yes. As long as that suited our goals, then it's a fine answer. What about the risk of losing 20% to make 9%? Maybe. It depends on your goals.

There Will Be Math. For the ten years ended 2015, the

total US stock market averaged about 9% returns. In two of those years, it lost more than 20%. Obviously it did better in other years and ends up with a 9% average for the past decade. Was it a smart investment to own the stock market? History would say yes. But who knew at the beginning? The best you could know is you risked significant loss in some years, but the historical average return was around a plus 9%. The last decade for the US stock market was actually pretty average if we use history as a guide. But there's no way to know that for sure at the beginning, all you can do is project your risk vs. return expectation and decide from there.

Final thought on getting started. There is considerable sentiment among the truly wealthy that risk-free return is all that matters. **Never Risk Principal** is an often heard piece of advice in families with multiple generations of wealth, and they only make investments with zero risk. We also lean in this direction, even though we grew up poor. The investing game is pretty well rigged in favor of the big guys, and taking risks frequently is a formula for losing.

However, never taking risk is much better advice for **staying** rich than it is for **getting** rich. To gain ground, we will have to take more risk than those already sitting on their pot of gold. However, by not being stupid about it, we will get higher returns while still keeping the idea of risk-free within reach. And when we do take risk, we are not stupid about it. You have to step very carefully through the minefield.

The DontBeStupid.club Summary:

- Step one is a deep understanding of risk vs. return.

- We choose investments based on our goal. Some goals demand we take high risks. Other goals call for more conservative choices.

- We need a deep understanding of our risk-free return baseline. Any risk we take has to have a return high enough above it for us to consider taking the added risk.

- Unless our goals are very modest, we will need to take some risks. But we will not be stupid about it.

4.
Now Consider Taxes

TAXES ENTER EVERY financial decision. It's inevitable. And they get into our investment decisions even more than anywhere else because investing is about making a profit. And if there's one thing that simply must be taxed to the maximum, it's profit. Sometimes we're astonished people feel motivated to make any profit at all. With no other choice it becomes the only game in town, but with tax rates that can hit 50%, and constantly changing, it sure takes some of the fun out of investing.

Seriously, the taxes on investment profits are so great that it kills many investments before they get started. The tax burden cuts the return so much it's just not worth the risk anymore. For this reason, tax-deferred accounts are the first choice for most investors. Specifically, 401k's and IRAs are the most common. And 529 college plans are a growth industry now too. There are others for specific circumstances, but the rules are largely the same with the only variables being who administers the account, the contribution limits, and when you can withdraw.

Tax-deferred does not mean tax-free. *Define the Target.* Tax-Deferred – Taxes are paid at a future date instead of the period when they are incurred. So you always pay your taxes, you just pay later instead of right now if investing in a deferred account.

Both tax-deferred and taxable accounts buy the same investments. The universe of choices is basically the same. In fact, it's not uncommon for an investor to have two accounts buying the same thing. One is the tax-deferred up to the government enforced contribution limit, and the other is the taxable account holding the remainder of invested money.

401ks are usually the best choice. But they are offered only through employers. If you are a sole proprietor or a partner in a company with no employees, then you can set up an Individual 401k. For everyone else, there are IRAs. In general, the only meaningful difference is the contribution limits are greater for a 401k. There are other arcane rules like you can borrow against a 401k but not your IRA, but *Simplify*. If you are following the DontBeStupid.club path, you are not borrowing against your investment account.

An employer match is a common fringe benefit attached to a 401k. If you have an employer that is generous with the matching, be certain to invest the maximum that gets matched. That is free money they are giving you, and virtually guarantees the investment is at least OK. 401k's are plagued by high fees and other ways to screw the employee participants. But if you get a generous employer match to your contribution, then that free money covers up a lot of other problems.

Taxes suck. If you are lucky enough to reside in places like Hong Kong, you don't get taxed on investment gains. We cannot help but comment that taxes impact investment far more than lowering or raising interest rates. It's pretty simple. People invest to make a profit. Taxes take away some of the profit. So higher taxes make the investment look less attractive. Changing interest rates doesn't matter as much. Smart investors are not borrowing much for their investment anyway.

> Side Note: lower interest rates are supposed to stimulate investment. It works a little, not a lot. For example, the theory is people buy more houses. But that's stupid. No new people are created by low interest rates, and people already live somewhere. What really happens is people buy more expensive houses, taking on greater debt while delivering greater profits to builders. Dubious value to an economy in that.

Think for Yourself. Hong Kong has never had interest rates as low as the USA or Euro zone. Yet investing remains strong. Hong Kong budget surpluses are so robust they are usually underestimated. That's right, budget surplus not budget deficit. As we write this book, Hong Kong has underestimated their surplus 8 years in a row. Every country could tax like Hong Kong. As a group, our politicians are just stupid.

The DontBeStupid.club Summary:

- Taxes are a significant burden on investments. It is always better to invest tax-deferred if possible.

- Some investments make sense ONLY when done in a tax-deferred account. The tax burden can be high enough to kill some choices.

- Other than the tax deferral, 401k's and IRA's operate pretty much the same as any other investment account. Taxable accounts just have taxes to pay as additional expense.

- Taxes are a choice made by governments.

5.
Step Three. Really Start.

OPEN AN ACCOUNT. Yep, its time and this is the next step. Make it a pretax or after tax account based on the previous chapter and your personal situation.

You may already have a 401k account through your employer. This can be a valuable fringe benefit if you are ready to invest. If you have an employer match, *Simplify*. Invest the amount in your 401k that your employer matches. The match is free money to you and it's a virtual certainty that it makes the return on investment a good one.

But do check out what kind of match you get. If it's company stock, then you need to move out of most of it as soon as possible. It is not smart to have too much of your money in one company's stock, especially if you work there too. If the company tanks, then you lose your job at the same time your investment loses value. It's like getting punched twice.

If you do not have an account through your employer, or if you have more money to invest than what will be matched in your 401K, then you're going to need an investment account somewhere so you can buy investments.

This is a very competitive arena with many high quality players. We are partial to Vanguard, which you already know if you read the dedication to this book. (You're not one of those insensitive types who skips over dedications. Right? Go read it right now if you skipped.) But we won't turn this into a sales pitch for Vanguard. Among other things, they're not paying us. Actually, that's one of the good things about Vanguard, they don't pay anyone to sell their products. How did a trillion dollars find them with no salesmen?

Most investing accounts at Vanguard can be funded with about $3,000. *Simplify*. If you don't have at least $3000, don't bother opening an investment account yet. It's not worth it. Invest in bulk purchases at the next big sale and fill up your pantry. If you save $300 on essentials for next year, your ROI on $3000 is 10%, tax-free, risk-free and no fees. That's a great investment.

But Vanguard is not the only good choice. There are other high quality operations out there that are a safe place for your investing account. Companies like Charles Schwab, TD Ameritrade, Scottrade, E-Trade, and Fidelity are all worthy of your consideration. And that list does not mention everyone. There are more, and we apologize to other quality organizations we did not mention. But *Simplify*. And go to Vanguard. (Sorry, we couldn't resist.)

All of them are anxious for your business. Just call or go online; you might be amazed at the level of service provided. That should give you some idea of how much profit is made selling investment products. They REALLY want your money. You'll think you are in customer service heaven. Especially if you've had to call your cable company recently...

One point we want to call to attention here. This list of account providers is NOT for brokers you'd choose to do a lot of stock trading. But frequent stock trading is not really investing even though some people like to call it that. *Don't Be Distracted*. Trading is a lot more like playing a casino game. Usually you lose, but you might win. The financial markets are very much like a casino, but with an even greater number of choices. Trading can be fun, and maybe even fun to write about. It's loaded with stupidity, but we're going to ignore it here. It's not investing.

Any company competing to hold our investing account must have a pristine history of honest and capable operations. It needs to be large enough to handle financial upheavals without disturbing us. In other words, if there's a "run on the bank" they are big enough to handle it without tapping into our money. And once we have identified some candidates worthy of our business, then we want low fees. Low fees are mandatory.

There Will Be Math. The total of all fees paid by investors has never been calculated. The mean salary for a "financial advisor" in the USA appears to be around $85,000. There are roughly 300,000 jobs in this category. That adds up to about $25 billion in annual compensation. So we know at least that much money is paid to people motivated to keep it complicated. Annually.

And that's only one part of the picture. The total number has to include more people and will be way higher. For example, mutual fund managers generally don't disclose their salaries. The average is reportedly around \$400,000 although that is skewed by the ridiculously high compensation of a relative few. Still, the total money sucked out of investor's pockets for these managers is quite large. As is the amount sucked out by all the trading fees from the brokers selling the various investments.

Follow the Money. Investment fees are a big business. One of the biggest in the world. There is a lot of motivation to keep you thinking they need to be paid. And stupid people will keep paying them. It's a growth industry.

We want to be fair. Nobody should work for free. Some investment fees are justified. Some people are actually doing valuable work and deserve to be paid. And we will gladly look at their products for potential investments. But the majority of fees are not necessary and only stupid people pay them. Doing the analysis is a little challenging, but not all that difficult.

Fees are the drag on all investments. Fees are why everyone is so anxious to service you. But whatever money we pay in fees is money that cannot be invested and generate any return for us. Ideally, there would be no fees at all and 100% of our money would generate return (like happens when paying down debt). But no one works for free so we have to expect some expenses if we want to buy investments. Fees are hidden everywhere. So we have to be diligent in our analysis.

Fees are part of every investment evaluation. Whatever return we are projecting for an investment, we have to subtract fees. A little earlier we mentioned the US stock market returned about 9% over the last 10 years. Unfortunately, no one actually got that much. Investors got what was left after their fees and expenses were subtracted from the 9%.

Let's choose this as the next example of an investment analysis. *There Will Be Math*. Let's say we've got that $10,000 to invest and we've decided to accept the risk vs. return we see in owning the US Stock Market for the next year. You can buy your own little piece of the entire market by putting your $10,000 into a "Total Stock Market" index fund (or ETF). You are now the proud owner of 0.000000033% of the US stock market.

You will get your share of how much the market goes up or down in the next year. You will also pay your fees to own it. Your profit is whatever is left after the fees. If you own the Vanguard product, your fees total 0.1% of dollars invested. $10 total for your $10,000 investment. If the market gains 9%, you will get back $890 return on your investment, $10 short of the full amount the market gained.

You can also buy this same product from many other sources. Some charge expense fees above 1%. Some even charge a sales fee to sell you the product in the first place (they call it a "load" as in "that's a load of crap"; we won't use a sales fee for this example, just know it would make things worse).

The 1% fee means $100 of expenses for our $10,000 invested. *There Will Be Math*. So instead of the $890 we got at Vanguard, we get $800. For the exact same investment. There is no variation in the risk vs. return we analyzed, only the fees are different. And by making a stupid choice, the buyers in this fund cost themselves 10% of their total return.

That is a real example, using a big bank everyone knows. We're not naming names because we don't want to piss off anyone so big. That would be stupid. But we hope the point is clear. You can choose to NOT buy from the high fee sellers, the same way you might shop for gasoline at a lower price.

By the way, that high fee fund we just discussed has over $1.5 billion in it. Good salesmen. And a lot of stupid investors. And it's not unusual either. There are thousands of similar examples we could make.

Now that we've illustrated the real world difference made by fees, this brings up another fundamental axiom about fees. The lower the expected return, the more important fees and expenses become. *There Will Be Math*. If we are buying that 3-month T-Bill we mentioned earlier and it's expected to return 0.15%, then we better hope our expenses are really low or it will end up costing us money to own it. Own it through that big bank we mentioned, and you will pay them more than it returns. Stupid.

OK, let's assume we did not buy any investments yet. We end this chapter with $10,000 in a low expense investing account. That money will be held in a money market account. It's just cash. And if we're lucky, the interest being paid to us on our cash account is at least enough to offset the fees for holding it. Back in the dark ages, like 2005, the yield on cash was closer to 3%. There was never any worry the yield on cash would not at least cover the expense of holding it.

Fast forward to the present. Interest rates on cash are so low that in some high fee stupid places, people are running negative, paying out for someone to hold their investing cash. It's a new concept, and would have been inconceivable just a few years ago. But definitely something to watch out for in the future. Large banks are already charging their business customers to hold cash. In most cases, they also charge a fee for accepting the cash deposit. It's gotten a little stupid.

The DontBeStupid.club Summary:

- Open an account with a strong and trustworthy company. (ahem... Vanguard... cough...)

- Minimizing fees is always a consideration. Fees can make some investments not worth owning at all.

- Be mindful of where you hold your cash.

6.
The Getting Started Summary

LET'S PAUSE FOR a short summary here. 75% of successful investing is about starting correctly. Once headed in the right direction, it's a lot easier getting where we want to go.

1) Be certain you're ready to invest. This is money you cannot use for any better purpose.

2) Have a very clear and deep understanding of the risk vs. return concept.

3) Know your risk-free return. This is the baseline for all risk vs. return evaluations.

4) Know your goal for the investment. The goal dictates certain choices as right or wrong.

5) Open an account with a high quality and low fee company like Vanguard.

If any of those five items is unclear, please go back over the preceding chapters. The following chapters assume an understanding of the above.

The DontBeStupid.club Summary:

- This was a summary. We don't need another one. So we'll tell a joke instead.

- Two new graduates walk into a bar. And start serving beers because it's the only job they can get.

7.
Stocks, Bonds and Mutual Funds

OK, WE HAVE to know the pieces in this game and understand how they move. If you listen to all the salespeople making their living selling investments, you think the universe is divided into Stocks, Bonds and Mutual Funds. Nothing could be further from the truth, of course, but these are the first and biggest group of investment choices that people consider. This is where most investors spend their entire life, usually making stupid choices.

Define the Target. Stock - A claim on the assets and earnings of a company.

Stock is frequently referred to as partial ownership in a corporation or Equity. *Don't Be Distracted.* That sounds good, but you get very few of the rights and privileges of an owner. Take your share of AT&T into headquarters and ask to use the executive bathroom. See how far you get. Any ownership delusions will be clarified for you quickly. What you really get with stock is the right to your proportionate share of whatever profits the board of directors decides to give shareholders. Understand that. You get whatever the board of directors wants to give you. Nothing more.

Define the Target. Bond – A debt investment wherein the investor lends money to the borrowing company.

Bonds are considered more conservative or "safer" than stocks because they are a legally enforceable debt. *Don't Be Distracted*. Most bonds available to investors have nothing backing them up beyond the company's promise to pay. Their perceived value is because they get paid ahead of stockholders. But that's not the same as the mortgage on your house. You will get no chance to repossess anything if the company misses their payments. The "senior" debt holders will dictate any payment restructuring. You will get whatever the bigger fish decide to give you. *Simplify*. A bond gets you paid ahead of stock, and behind everyone else. It's only as good as the company's promise to pay.

Define the Target. Mutual Fund - A company that pools money from multiple investors and invests in stocks, bonds and other assets. Each investor owns shares that represent his or her proportionate claim on the assets.

Don't Be Distracted. Mutual funds come in an unlimited variety and are sold with unlimited claims. Fun Fact: There are over 7,000 mutual funds available for purchase while there are only 4,000 stocks traded on the NYSE and NASDAQ combined. Flawed logically but funny anyway.

Let's immediately *Simplify*. You have no business investing in individual stocks or bonds unless you bring the same tools to the game as the sharks. That is possible today if you want to make it a full-time career, or at least a very serious hobby. If you want to put all your energy into it, learn and practice with the tools, you might get almost good enough to compete with Goldman Sachs.

Being almost able to compete with the sharks sounds like a stupid investment goal to us. We have better things to do with our time than try to get almost as good as Goldman Sachs. So we only rarely buy stocks or bonds.

Everybody knows somebody who made a killing in a stock. We also know trees that got hit by lightning. It happens. But the trees don't write books or go on TV and talk about their strategy. Only stupid people think lottery winners are brilliant investors. Don't believe anything you hear from someone who only talks about their success. It's just like the guy leaving the casino who only remembers the jackpot he hit on the way out. Somehow all the other losing bets are not part of the strategy.

Now we're going to state a simple truth here. We are good at analysis. Professionals pay us to do it for them. But we can't beat the sharks at their own game and we don't try. We almost never recommend individual stocks. You know who else should not recommend stocks? Pretty much every person with a TV show. Go ahead and check their track records. Their stock picks are below average even before you take out the expenses required to make their trades.

That means you don't have the tools or expertise to do anything except get lucky picking a stock. And just like gambling in a casino, you will lose more often than you win. *Follow the Money*. Entire TV networks and many investment companies are built on people's desire to play in this game. There are programs and books and TV shows and advisors and clubs and on and on, selling this fantasy to investors, the notion that they can be successful stock traders, is a very big business. And it would shrink dramatically if enough people just figured out they are stupid for playing in the shark's game.

Even more importantly, the sharks would suffer if enough people stopped being stupid. They need to eat the little fish to stay so big. If little fish are not available, the sharks must eat each other, or at least go on a diet. But thanks to the relentless marketing machine, there are always plenty of little fish coming along. Everybody is programmed to buy stocks and bonds. Poor stupid little fish... But tasty!

The government is even telling companies to automatically enroll employees in 401k's now. It's almost un-American to suggest people should not buy these investments. To be fair, many of these are OK investments, but institutionalizing the buying without the investor understanding what they're doing is a very bad precedent to set for a society. *Follow the Money*. Is there any doubt why the government would make rules like this? Who profits? Don't be stupid.

There is only one way to swim with the sharks, and that is to be part of a bigger fish. You know what happens if Carl Icahn walks into AT&T and asks to use the executive bathroom? We'll let you work that one out for yourself. We'll just add that the monogrammed toilet paper will be there before he's finished. Carl only invests his own money now. We cannot be part of that big fish. But we can join William Danoff, the guy who runs Fidelity Contrafund. Or even better, join F. William McNabb the current CEO of Vanguard. The company founded by John Bogle manages over $3 trillion of investing money today. That's three Trillion dollars. Very big fish. Sharks beware.

Simplify. Mutual funds are the only stock and bond investing vehicle worth considering for the average investor. You do not want to spend the time to get fluent with PE, ROE, ROI, IRR, Debt to Equity, Interest coverage, asset turnover and on and on... an infinite parade of financial calculations people use in their attempt to gain the advantage over someone else. When you choose the mutual fund path, all that work is done for you by people who do it for a living. Some of them are good at it, and because of the economy of scale you get their service very cheaply.

Define the Target. Economy of Scale – Savings in per unit cost gained through an increased level of production.

What that means is the investment analysis gets done once by the fund management. But thousands of investors are in the fund so the cost is spread among so many people that the cost to each investor becomes very low. That's how mutual funds work. A lot of people pool their investment dollars and the expenses related to making the investments become very low.

And if we do just a little math to compare risk vs. return, we can *Simplify* again. Out of the 7,000 mutual funds available to choose from, there are only about 100 worth considering. So what begins as an overwhelming universe of investing choices, that giant casino called the stock market, it really can be reduced to about 100 mutual funds. And we're being generous, we could make that list as short as 10 or 20, but we would neglect some truly well-run funds and good young money managers who someday might be the best.

But applying just two of our principles, *There Will Be Math* and *Simplify*, we get down to 100 worthy choices pretty quickly. It's just math and kind of boring to read. Very repetitive as you might expect when rejecting 6900 similar investment products. So we are not going to put all that math in this book. Back in the "Getting Started" section, we showed you the fee difference between two funds selling the same market index. Same investment, one was just a more expensive place to buy it. Using that same type of analysis will eliminate most of the 7,000 available mutual fund choices. Our choices for the best are in the Bonus Content section of our website (http://dontbestupid.club/investing-bonus-content/top-10-mutual-funds/).

Follow the Money. The reason for the other 98.5% of the choices to exist is simply to extract more profit from you. That's actually why it's easy to eliminate so many of them. *Don't Be Distracted*. Keep your focus on your goal, and the risk vs. return that's acceptable, and you do not even need to think about the very great majority of investment choices out there. They add unnecessary risk and costs that drag down your returns. Less return and more risk is the perfect definition of stupid investing.

Mutual funds are where you will invest the vast majority of any money you put towards stocks and bonds. And only the best mutual funds need to be considered. Most can be ignored.

OK, we said we RARELY buy stocks. We will now give you an example of when it might be a good idea. This is a real life example, something we really did.

Learn from History. One night after work we tried a new restaurant in the neighborhood. It blew us away. Far better than the typical experience in their price range. We went home that night and looked up the company. It turned out to be an expansion of a company with a few other locations. Only about 5 of them. And it turned out to be a publicly traded company. We could buy their stock if we wanted to.

We proceeded to evaluate their story. Turned out, the owners had been in the food business a long time. They had owned fast food franchises, about 60 of them, and decided to pivot (change strategic direction). When they sold off the fast food chain, their total revenue fell sharply. And the stock price plummeted. There were a few other challenges but, in our opinion, they had very well qualified management launching a new concept that we thought was great.

So we bought in at under $2 per share. And we ate at our location at least once a month, mainly because it was great, but also because we got to keep watch on our investment. If it ever was not great, we would have gotten out of the investment faster than anyone else could have known. But it was always great. We sold it all about 8 years later at $9 per share. And in the end, we made a lot more money on the investment than we'd spent in the restaurant enjoying ourselves. Sweet!

The company was later bought out and trades today as J. Alexander Holdings. And if you can find the company history prior to the buy-out, you can track down when we started eating there. Not exactly fascinating. But a chance to *Learn from History*.

The point is this. Sometimes, due to personal experience, you can do better than the biggest fish. But *Trust Common Sense*. You know when you really have an insider look. If you are a regular customer, that's one way. Another might be due to your unique expertise in a specific area. But know this: the big boys always understand the numbers much better than you and they can manipulate the numbers to their advantage. Your specific knowledge of the business must be so much better that it compensates for the financial disadvantages.

One more word about specific knowledge. Specific knowledge does not mean acting on a hot tip from an "insider".

Define the Target. Insider – a person within an organization with access to information unavailable to others.

"Insider trading" is illegal. And stupid. The fact is, 99% of these "hot tips" are losers anyway. It really doesn't even need to be illegal for the average investor. Most insider tips are so stupid to begin with the investor losses are punishment enough. But bottom line, you are REALLY not qualified to break the law when investing. Even people who are real professionals at it get caught occasionally. It doesn't stop all of them, so don't feel too good about it. Insider trading goes on all the time. It's one more reason you really don't want to swim alone among the sharks.

The DontBeStupid.club Summary:

- You cannot compete with the professionals in trading stocks and bonds.

- For the vast majority of your stock and bond purchases, mutual funds will be your best choice.

- With specific insight due to unique circumstances or expertise, on very rare occasions you can gain an advantage over the big boys.

- Specific knowledge does not mean "insider" information. Stay legal. Don't be stupid.

8.
Picking Mutual Funds

AS WITH EVERY other opportunity in the investment sales world, whole businesses have been built up around helping you pick "the right" mutual funds. *Think for Yourself.* Evaluating mutual funds is not that difficult. We're going to teach you how to do it right now.

First Things First. Mutual funds come in two basic flavors, Actively Managed and Index.

Define the Target. Actively Managed – A fund where the manager or management teams makes decisions about what investments to buy for the fund.

Define the Target. Index Fund – An investment portfolio assembled to match a financial market index.

For example, Standard and Poor's is an American financial services company. S&P publishes their index of the 500 leading companies. It's their index, so they pick who's in it. Generally speaking, it's the 500 most widely owned companies traded on the NYSE or NASDAQ, and the companies in it represent about 80% of the value in the total US stock market. It's a good benchmark for large USA company stocks.

The Vanguard 500 Index fund tracks the S&P 500 stock index. In effect, the fund buys all the stocks in that index in the same proportion as the index weights them. If the S&P 500 index goes up 10%, then the Vanguard fund goes up 10%. And the investor in the fund gets the profit, after expenses.

Index funds are sometimes referred to as passively managed funds but that is not accurate. They require skilled management, just not people picking the investments. People selling actively managed funds will call them passive because, well come on, wouldn't you rather buy something active than passive? *Don't Be Distracted.* Changing names is just used as a sales gimmick.

Done right, Index funds have lower costs than actively managed funds. And if the index fund tracks its benchmark accurately, then it will deliver that return at a lower cost than an actively managed fund.

For example, in the case of Vanguard 500 Index, the expenses are about 0.1%, or $10 per $10,000 invested. Fees for the typical actively managed large cap stock fund are over 1%, or $100 for every $10,000. So the index fund begins with an expense advantage that any active manager must overcome by being better than average. And that is very difficult to do for any extended period of time. Why?

In every trade, there is a buyer and a seller. Each thinks they are making the right move. One thinks the investment is a good buy, and the other would rather sell it. Only one of them is right. Active fund managers have little or no advantage over each other when it comes to skills and tools, so their wins and losses tend to balance out over time. Like flipping a coin. But their expenses are always higher.

If 10 great poker players sit down at the same table, luck is the only variable that matters. Luck is just a statistical probability, and over time, luck evens out. All of those players will lose eventually if they have to pay expenses. And you may flip a coin and get heads four times in a row, but you are not a genius. It's just random chance. It's the same with professional stock pickers. Eventually, it all evens out, and they lose their expenses.

Note, we must repeat something we said earlier. You are at an extreme disadvantage trying to compete with either fund managers or great poker players. Playing in their game with them is stupid.

There Will Be Math. More than 90% of actively managed large-cap stock funds fail to beat the 500 index over a 10-year period. It's the inevitable mathematic conclusion. If you go back for longer periods of time, the odds of picking a winner are even worse. You will find ridiculous amounts of sales pressure claiming otherwise. Ignore it. Toward the end of this chapter we'll talk more about sales bullshit.

Comparing any mutual fund performance to an index built on the same investment goals is always a good first step.

All mutual funds are built from stocks (equity), bonds (debt), and cash. They are sliced, diced, combined and recombined in many different ways, frequently with expensive sounding names, until you have over 7000 mutual funds to choose from. Most are just a marketing gimmick designed to generate fees at your expense.

Simplify. We don't have to address all the marketing

gimmicks as long as we understand that in the bottom line analysis, there is nothing you can do to those three basic elements that makes them more profitable than they are fundamentally. If a stock goes up, the best way to get your share of the profit is to own it with as little expense as possible. Added complications might sound great, but *Don't Be Distracted*. They don't add any value. But they do add expenses.

So we want to limit our consideration to low-fee funds, usually index funds, with simple structures. Some funds are all stock, some all bond, and some are just money markets holding cash. Some funds hold a balance of all three elements. You do not ever want to consider anything more complicated. More complications equals more profit to the sellers, less to the investors.

Your profit from investing comes in two forms: income paid to you for owning the investment, and price appreciation in the investment.

An income-producing stock is one that pays a dividend. *Define the Target*. Dividend – A sum of money paid by a company to its shareholders. Roughly 80% of the S&P 500 stocks pay dividends. That percentage goes down as you get into smaller companies. Dividends on stocks, and interest payments on bonds, are regular periodic payments made to owners of those securities. Those are called "income" and you get those just by owning the investment.

When you sell the investment, if the price is higher than when you bought it, then you have profit from the price appreciation. That's called a capital gain. If you buy at $10 and sell at $12 you have a $2 capital gain.

Prices go up and down based on the supply and demand in the market. "Buy low and sell high" just means generate capital gains.

So the two ways you profit from investing are income and capital gains.

In general, investors build an investment portfolio pursuing both income and capital gains in some ratio that suits their goals and temperament. The more risk-averse investors buy more income investments, and aggressive investors buy more stocks for capital gains. Everyone can find a balance that suits them.

The final consideration in choosing a mutual fund is management. We know we want a low-fee fund consisting of the simple elements that match up to our goals for income and/or capital gains. Who will deliver that to us at the best price? This is where you want management you can rely on. It's not about who did great last year. Better to choose someone who's done pretty well for 10 years. The "stars" tend to fade in and out from one year to the next. Track records that last 10 years or more start to get more reliable. You will find one of our easy choices at the end has delivered since 1929.

OK, now you have all the elements. And more than 7,000 mutual funds to evaluate. *Simplify*. All funds must disclose their expenses in a prospectus that must be given to you before you buy. Be sure to read it. Eliminate everything with fees over 1% annually or management on the job less than 5 years. 10 years is even better. Eliminate anything that charges a sales load (aka the load of crap). Eliminate anything an advisor tries to sell you if they get a commission or kickback of any kind for making the sale. And eliminate anything not backed by a reputable company like Vanguard. The remaining list is now much shorter than 7,000.

Now look for the "best of breed". We like to start at Vanguard because that's very efficient. They usually win. Sometimes they come in second or third, but the difference is so small it's not worth chasing. So when looking for a fund to track the S&P 500 index, we choose the Vanguard 500 Index. It tracks the index perfectly, has very low fees and is backed by a company with an unequaled reputation. And now we can eliminate from our list all the other funds that compete in that segment. Our list gets shorter again.

Most simple bond funds will be won by Vanguard due to low fees. If you want a fund that owns US Treasuries, there isn't any way to beat a Vanguard Index in that area.

Keep up this exercise and, in the end, you will find maybe 10 or 20 funds that are worth thinking about. That daunting universe of 7,000 choices when we started is now reduced to a short menu of selections.

The differences tend to be very small when you're down to looking at only the best. Then you have to consider the conveniences. For example, as we write this, the Schwab 500 Index fund is undercutting Vanguard's fee by about 2/100 of one percent. And that's great; competition is good for us investors. But that's just $2 difference annually on a $10,000 investment. It's just not worth the expense and inconvenience to chase it. Plus, *Learn from History*. Vanguard wins in the long term. Their fees have been stable longer, and their commitment not to pay any salesmen has been in place since the beginning.

So *Don't Be Distracted*. If the differences are irrelevant, don't chase them. This applies in the other direction too. If you're already a happy Schwab account holder, don't chase funds somewhere else unless you're certain it's really worth it. Many companies run promotions occasionally where they waive fees for a while and claim to be the cheapest. *Learn from History*. All special sales end and the prices go back to normal sooner or later.

We don't want to sound like a sales pitch for Vanguard, but there is one fact investors should be aware of in their decision-making process. Vanguard is unique in the investment world in that it's a non-profit company. Vanguard is owned by the owners of its mutual funds. There are no other owners trying to make a profit off us. *Trust Common Sense*. With no owner's profits to pay out, Vanguard has a built-in advantage when it comes to fees. Services are delivered at cost. This makes it very unlikely another company can deliver lower fees over any sustained period of time.

The DontBeStupid.club Summary:

- Picking Mutual Funds is a process of elimination.

- The vast majority of the 7,000 choices are just higher cost duplicates of better choices.

- Reliable management and low fees are the most important considerations.

- It's tough to beat Vanguard's expenses due to their unique structure as investor-owned.

9.
Real Estate

NOT ALL INVESTMENTS are stocks, bonds and mutual funds. The next big category is real estate. And here's a little investing secret. This is actually the biggest category. More millionaires have made their money investing in real estate than any other investment choice. In general, **active** real estate investing has worked out far better than stocks and bonds for the ordinary investor.

The problem is real estate requires work. Active means you work at it. Passive real estate investors are not any better off than stock and bond investors. But people who buy property and fix it up, or buy income property like apartments or commercial property to rent out, these investors can do very well for themselves. But it takes a little work.

It is beyond the scope of this book to go heavy into the evaluation of specific real estate investments. If you're already into cap rates, NNN leases, and IRR then hopefully you're only reading our book for its entertainment value. If you're involved in those and don't understand them, well... we hope you got lucky. Feel free to visit our website and email us if you need help.

The main purpose of this chapter is to alert investors

that there are excellent investment choices that have no connection to the stock market. And although there are far too many realtors around, none is barraging you with the "Buy!" message of the Wall Street sales machine. People just don't think about this investment choice the same way as their 401k. But they should. It is frequently a better choice for your investment dollars.

Here is a perfect example anyone can consider. Let's assume your financial situation says you're ready to buy a house. One choice you could make is to buy a duplex, or even a four flat. You live on site in your own home, but also manage your rental units for income. A variation on this theme might be to buy your neighbor's house when it goes on sale and rent it out for income. The point is you manage your investment directly.

You do have to put in some effort to be a good real estate investor, but it's not that difficult to manage your own property when you live in it or it's right across the street. And on a small scale like this, the skills required are not much different than owning your own home. Beyond common sense and knowing a decent lawyer who can help you out when someone doesn't pay, you don't need much else. Many people get fluent enough with the law so they don't even need the lawyer.

Real estate investing is one area where you can consider some debt. For example, if you can buy a duplex, live in one half, and the rent you collect on the other half covers the debt payment, then you've got a pretty good investment situation.

Think of the above example in the context of retirement

investing. 15 or 30 years down the road, the debt is paid off. You have no debt but still collect the rent. And in general rent increases with inflation so your buying power is preserved. This is a great retirement plan, with no one else collecting fees from your investment. You can forget everything you heard about the right mix of bonds and stocks for your age, etc. You invested in a better answer.

Again, the main purpose of this chapter is to alert the potential investor that opportunities exist beyond the mainstream thinking, and real estate is the biggest opportunity. As much as we like Vanguard, we see less risk and more predictable return in owning a paid off four flat in a solid neighborhood than any mutual fund they can offer.

The DontBeStupid.club Summary:

- Real estate is actually the biggest investment opportunity available. It makes more people rich than the stock market.

- Small scale do-it-yourself real estate investors can build wealth doing only a little more work than owning their own house would be on its own.

10.
Commodities

COMMODITY INVESTING RUNS through hot and cold cycles depending on the sales machine and perceived profit to be made by fleecing the investors. We're sorry if that sounds too adversarial, but it's just a reality. Virtually all small investors lose money when betting on commodities. And yes, we said betting. That's all it is.

Define the Target. Betting – The act of gambling on the outcome of an unpredictable event.

Define the Target. Commodity – a raw material or primary product that can be bought or sold.

Now, if you believe you have some special knowledge convincing you that copper is going up, by all means place the bet. Buy copper futures. But be honest. Exactly how special is your knowledge?

When thinking about commodities, it helps to remember why these markets exist in the first place. Ever heard the phrase "hedge your bets"?

Define the Target. Hedge – An investment designed to limit the risk of future price movements.

Commodities markets were formed to service companies that have a legitimate business need to hedge. One good example of this is airlines. Jet fuel is a very volatile commodity. *Define the Target*. Volatile – prone to changing rapidly and unpredictably. Jet fuel prices are volatile.

But airlines need to know how to price their tickets more than a few gas tanks worth in advance. So airlines will buy their fuel for the next 6 months on the commodities market. Someone else takes their order, and takes the risk of prices moving against them. Basically, the seller is betting the price will go down, and the buyer is betting the price will go up. The contract may last longer or shorter, we just picked 6 months to make the example. But wherever buyer and seller can agree, a contract can be made. And hedging fuel prices is smart business for airlines. They need to know their costs are fixed for at least a little while.

If you understand that above paragraph, you now understand commodities. Totally and completely. Please feel confident in a conversation with any expert using bigger words.

Now the Wall Street profit machine and the programmed little fish investors enter the commodities picture. You can get rich in commodities. They can go up a lot, and faster than stocks or bonds. There's no reason only Southwest Airlines should be able to buy futures in jet fuel. We all have equal rights to gain that wealth!

Unfortunately, commodities can go down a lot faster than stocks and bonds too.

So here's the fundamental question you have to ask yourself. If Southwest Airlines is selling jet fuel, why are you buying? Which one of you knows more about the likely price of jet fuel 6 months from now? We know we'd bet on Southwest, but they are not sharing their bet with us. And that is why we do not trade commodities.

Gold is considered a commodity and deserves some special attention. Everyone is invited to invest in gold as a hedge against paper currency failure. Here's our take.

Define the Target. Gold – Atomic number 79, a soft malleable yellow metallic element.

That's all gold is, an element on the periodic table. You cannot eat it or live in it or grow food on it. You really cannot do much with gold except look at it or sell it. Gold has no intrinsic value; it has no value other than whatever people will pay for it.

We do not believe gold is a hedge against the failure of paper currency (assuming you own one of the majors). People evaluate these things inside boundaries that are not real. If a major economy meltdown occurs, it is highly unlikely the organized markets valuing gold will be functioning normally. You will own atomic number 79 but with no market readily available to trade it. It will be really hard to monetize atomic number 79 in any immediately beneficial way. Gold won't buy shit if you need a gun to get food. And that is the opposite of what a hedge is supposed to accomplish.

The major currencies are US Dollars and Euros. If you own anything else, gold might make sense as a hedge. It is quite possible the Japanese yen could fail and the people of Japan would still get value for their gold instead. Same thing can be said for China's yuan or even Canadian dollars. In those cases, gold is a reasonable choice as a hedge against currency failure. Note, the Canadian dollar is among the world's soundest currencies. We just used it for example because it's a small component of the world's currency and its failure would not be statistically significant.

But if you live in the USA or Eurozone, forget it. If those currencies fail, then there won't be a way to readily monetize your gold. And they won't accept it at the grocery store either. There are better hedges out there to reduce your risk. Gold doesn't even correlate with inflation, so it's not a good choice even if you're just worried about your currency devaluing instead of failing.

By the way, if you buy gold just as a hedge against inflation, that's a stupid investment. It's part of a mainstream sales pitch with no basis in reality. *Think for Yourself*. There is near zero correlation between gold prices and inflation. A better choice for inflation hedge would be US Treasury Inflation Protected Securities or TIPS as they are called (clever or stupid name?). Real estate is also a good inflation hedge.

Gold prices are volatile, as are most commodities in general. And if you like the action, take some shots on commodities. But do it with money you'd spend in a casino. Don't kid yourself and call it investing.

The DontBeStupid.club Summary:

- The average investor is stupid to bet on commodities. It is just gambling.
- The big players have the edge. They are likely to know more about the commodity than you.

11.
Combinations and Derivatives

WE WILL HAVE a brief chapter here to talk about something everyone hears about, and almost no one understands. No one reading this should have any reason for looking at these products in their investing life. But people will try to sell them to you.

Define the Target. Derivative – Something based on another source.

When you hear the term "derivative" applied to investments, all it means is that the product being sold is some other product that's been modified. Usually, this involves combining two or more products, but it can also mean a single product has been divided. This is what happens with a "zero coupon security". These are usually a bond derivative where the interest payments have been stripped off and sold separately from the principle repayment. Don't worry about it, you have no reason to ever buy one.

At the end of every analysis, all derivatives are just combinations of stocks and bonds, maybe with a little real estate, and occasionally some insurance in there too. There is nothing complicated about these products other than breaking them down into their simpler components. For the seller, the more obscure the better. For the buyer, this just means added fees.

There Will Be Math. The underlying investment products will return whatever they return, whether contained within a derivative or not. There is added work done to create these products and added fees to pay for that work. These added expenses are borne by the same underlying investment products you can buy directly. The return from these investments is not going to change, but the fees paid to own them in a derivative are higher. And usually A LOT higher.

The average investor has no need for any of these products. You will hear terms like: futures, warrants, zero's, options, swaps, strips, tints, variable annuities, CDO's, CDS's and many more. These are all derivatives. The typical investor has no legitimate use for these products.

The layering of fees makes all of them too expensive. The risk for the return they offer cannot compete with just buying the underlying non-modified products. There are no added fees for modifications if you just buy the components instead of the derivative. And the perceived benefits to derivatives are virtually always an emotional appeal. The typical investor has no reason to pay the fees to participate in any of these products.

Businesses have legitimate uses for various kinds of derivative products. But derivatives are a zero-sum game, meaning for every winner there must be an equal loser. Plus, the extra fees to create the products must be paid too. Individual investors are pulled into this game to be the stupid ones, the losers. Do not be one of them.

The DontBeStupid.club Summary:

- Leave derivatives of all kind to the businesses with legitimate needs

- and the losers who trade with them.

12.
Alternate Investments

THERE ARE MANY other potential investments to consider. People invest in art, wine, antiques, tulip bulbs and a host of other diversions.

It is beyond the scope of this book to get heavily into evaluating these various investments. The main purpose here is to broaden everyone's understanding of investment to include all the possibilities out there.

And we can offer certain universal rules. The value of any investment is going to be determined by the demand for it. How much do other people want what you are holding?

It is not wrong to buy a piece of art that you like. But do not fool yourself into thinking it's an investment unless you've applied the basic investing principles we covered earlier. What is your goal, what is the risk, and what is your anticipated return? If you cannot answer those questions, then you better be buying that painting because it looks good on your wall.

We love wine. Some people have very valuable wine cellars. But it's impossible for us to think about wine as an investment. Not many bottles last longer than 6 months around our house. If we don't drink them by then, we've probably gifted them to someone else.

One of our favorite examples of an alternate investment is Gene Siskel buying the white suit John Travolta wore in Saturday Night Fever. It was at a charity auction and Gene paid $2,000 for it in 1978, and he even got Travolta to autograph the lining. Siskel said it was a "no-brainer". There was only one, and it was destined to be iconic. Gene has passed on, but the suit sold in 1995 for $145,000. That is the definition of an alternative investment.

For those not familiar with the reference to tulip bulbs *Learn from History.* There was a point in time around 1635 where tulip bulbs were trading for the equivalent of roughly $2,500 today. Obviously, there was no USA then and no US Dollars. This investing activity was taking place in Holland and the money used was the Florin. Some people got rich investing in tulip bulbs. And when the market crashed, some people got very poor.

As with all investments having no intrinsic value, tulip bulb investing was just about supply and demand. The same thing is true for wine or Andy Warhol paintings. Alternative investments are tough to evaluate. For most people, it comes down to just buying something they like and maybe they get lucky too.

The DontBeStupid.club Summary:

- Alternative investments exist but to truly be an investment they must be evaluated the same as another investment.

- Otherwise, you're just buying something to look at. Or drink.

13.
Investing in Yourself

ONE OF THE best investments you can make is in yourself. Starting your own business can be the single best investment opportunity offered to anyone.

It is beyond the scope of this book to give too much advice on starting your own business. We have a book coming out soon on that topic, it might even be published by the time you are done reading this.

For purposes of this book, we want to make the potential investor aware that sometimes the best stock you can buy is the one you create yourself. Once you start a business, your stock is evaluated the same way as everyone else's right up to and including the biggest companies in the world. The difference is, you know more about your stock than anyone else possibly could know. Is it a good investment?

If it is, then pour all your efforts into it. Ignore anyone telling you otherwise. You will hear a lot of advice telling you to diversify your risk. Ignore it. *Learn from History*. A very rich person once said, "put all your eggs in one basket and then watch that basket carefully." That was Andrew Carnegie. It was later used by Warren Buffet. We'll leave it to you to decide which one of those investors you'd rather emulate.

For those of you interested in trivia, the amount of

money Carnegie gave to charity, adjusted for inflation, is more than Buffet's entire net worth today. Just the amount Carnegie gave away. Both are worthy role models, but Carnegie has the benefit of more historical context and was truly amazing. Carnegie, as in Carnegie Hall, Carnegie Mellon University. We really do admire Buffet, and the Gates Foundation, and John Mackey and conscious capitalism and similar uses of personal fortunes today. But Carnegie's "the Gospel of Wealth" from the 1880's is the mother of all capitalist manifestos. It's a "must-read" for anyone who thinks they understand capitalism. Most people really don't. But that's another book...

One piece of universal advice we want to give every potential investor. If you feel passionate about starting your own business, then go for it. Don't be stupid, do it with critical thinking, but if you do it smart then you cannot make a better investment than betting on yourself. However, know in advance it is harder than you think.

Much harder than you think, unless you get lucky. The entrepreneurs you see grabbing the headlines are not the normal story. Those are the very rare stories that make great news. And the irony is, in most cases they are just smart people who stumbled into something. They got lucky. The more normal story is different. It's an idea coupled with passion, followed by a long struggle with a lot of ups and downs and sleepless nights. And in the end, if you work hard and get a little lucky, you do very well.

We're speaking from experience here. We've started several businesses, created hundreds of jobs (not thousands, but hundreds...) and spent many sleepless nights fighting the battles of small business. But if you have the appetite for it, your own stock is the best investment you can make.

The DontBeStupid.club Summary:

- Consider investing in your own business. No one will be able to value the stock better than you.

- Don't be afraid to put all your eggs in your own basket.

14.
Retirement Investing

THE HOLY GRAIL. We get to do whatever we want and still have money for the rest of our lives. That's the dream used to sell millions of retirement investments. The truth is a bit different.

Think for Yourself. For many of us, there is no desire to retire. Ever. What's going to be more fun than what we're doing right now? This whole idea of saving for retirement is a complete waste of time for some people.

But if you hate your job, then by all means retire from it as soon as possible. But even then, you may not want to just go fishing every day. Maybe retirement isn't really the right goal. Maybe just a change of scenery is the right answer. Again, this notion that you need to save enough money to not work for 30 years is just stupid for many people.

OK, but for some people the idea of going fishing every day sounds great. And yes, a lifelong vacation might be pleasant if done properly. But it probably isn't as easy as all the advertising you see makes it sound. *Don't Be Distracted.* Stop thinking of this special thing called "retirement" and just call it what it really is, a lifelong vacation. And vacations cost money. One lasting the rest of your life is going to be very expensive. That should come as no surprise to anyone using critical thinking.

How much do you need to retire? "Your number" and ideas like that, and all the products that will make that number work for you, they oversimplify a pivotal decision in life. Can I take a vacation forever? At this point, you have only one good choice. *There Will Be Math*. You have to figure it out.

The rest of your life, or the next 30 years, whichever comes first. That's a frequent dilemma when you're retirement planning. How much money do you need to be on vacation the rest of your life?

First, let's figure out if you're ready to retire. If you've handled your money as we advised in "Don't Be Stupid about Money", then you will have no debt when it's time to retire. Still have debt? Didn't read our book or didn't listen to us? Still owe money? Don't retire. You are not ready. Sorry if that sounds cruel, but it's just reality. If you have debt, you are not ready to retire. How are you going to vacation forever and owe people money?

There are ways to eliminate debt if you really want to retire.

A common situation for many people thinking about retirement is to have some equity in a house that also still has mortgage debt. OK, sell the house and buy whatever the equity can afford. For example, if you owe $100,000 on your house and can get $250,000 for it, then sell it and buy something for $150,000. Now you are debt free. Done. Retire.

Actually, depending on circumstances, you may even

buy something for $100,000 and use the remaining $50K for something else necessary to retire. Like paying off other debts. Debt equals no retirement. What you can actually pay for is all you can afford.

This is not what people thinking about retirement want to hear. And it's not going to generate big fees either. But it's the right answer.

There are a lot of "retirement planners" collecting fees who will hate our answer. And there will be all kinds of emotional arguments about how you shouldn't have to give up your beloved home. You are entitled to a retirement. A lot of emotional bullshit will be hurled your way so you can hear what you want to hear. This will be followed by "strategies" you can adopt to keep buying what you cannot really afford. And all of them involve you staying hooked on the drug that got us here in the first place: debt.

The least destructive "strategies" will require working longer so you can keep paying interest on that debt. And if it means that much to you, then you should keep working. Like we said, you're not ready for retirement. But don't pay fees or other product expenses for someone else to tell you that. Just keep earning and pay off the debts as soon as possible, and then actually retire.

More destructive "strategies" will sell you more debt to replace the current debt. "Reverse Mortgages" are being sold for this purpose now. Just reverse all the work you've done paying down your home mortgage, and now let it go up instead. Your debt is increasing as you age, and they are collecting more and more interest from you as you get older. But hey! You can retire and stay in your beloved home. *Trust Common Sense*. That's exactly as stupid as it sounds. And *Follow the Money*. It generates great fees for the lenders on some very low-risk loans. And when you have to move, you've lost your equity to debt.

For most people, they will never be a better sales target than at the time of retirement. They have a large chunk of money, and they are willing to spend it to get all of their retirement dreams fulfilled. If that describes you, just hang a bullseye on your back. And get ready to see a lot of pictures of happy old people sailing around the world and giving each other presents.

Don't Be Distracted. There are many predatory products for sale to help you avoid retirement answers you don't want to hear. Remember, everywhere you bleed money the world hangs a bucket. And the most sinister in the world are the ones targeting retirees. They have the least conscience among any of the sharks. Critical thinking is our weapon against these unsavory creatures.

Don't Be Distracted. Ignore the emotional appeals. You are entitled to nothing but what you've earned. You don't really need to sail around the world and give people pearl necklaces. And you don't need to keep your beloved home. *Think for Yourself*. What has made you happy before? Home is wherever you are happy sleeping. And you do not sleep happily with debt in retirement. You can only afford whatever retirement you can actually pay for. Get over it. No emotional decisions allowed.

And if you can find a way to live happily for 30 years without working, CONGRATULATIONS! That is one hell of an achievement no matter where you call home. Maybe you will canoe on the nearest lake as opposed to sailing the world. So what? Enjoy a debt free life wherever that may take you. You have paid in full and are on vacation forever. Well done!

When you clear out all the emotional clutter, nothing is simpler than a retirement budget. You have no debt, you have nothing to save up for, no kids to pay for (you have stopped paying for your kids by now, right? Think of kids like debt, you have to get rid of them before you can really retire).

All you have to pay for in retirement is your living expenses. And your budget will stay that simple as long as you continue to think about money critically and do not pay for chasing dreams.

No matter how simple, we do have to pay the expenses for as long as we live. That can be a little tricky. None of us really knows how long we will have those living expenses. But there is one universal concept that applies to all of us, you cannot run out of money. Survival is the most important budget consideration. Options to generate new income when you're 95 years old are a lot more limited than when you're 60.

More than any other time in life, this is when **Never Risk Principal** should guide everyone. Whatever you have, think just like the very wealthy and **Never Risk Principal**.

And don't be afraid of a part time job. That is not failure, it's just smart retirement. *Think for Yourself.* TV sucks and life will get boring anyway. You might as well have a little income to help with the budget. Find something you like to do and get paid for it.

The universal concepts shared in this chapter apply to everyone. But there is no single best strategy for addressing those unknown years of living expenses. Just be sure and retire with no debt and a very simple budget. And do not buy any of the predatory products promising to fulfill your dreams for a fee. Just enjoy whatever you can afford to pay for.

The DontBeStupid.club Summary:

- Retirement is not for everyone. In fact, it's for a lot less people than realize it. And all those people can ignore all the noise around saving for something they don't even care about.

- Retirement is a dream used to sell investment products. In reality it's just another vacation and your investment approach doesn't change.

- You cannot truly retire with debt. You are always working if you're paying interest to someone else.

- This is no time to dream. Enjoy whatever you can really pay for and don't buy anything sold to your emotions.

15.
Trusts and Estate Planning

ESTATE PLANNING IS an area where professionals can really help. The rules change frequently and the steps can be complicated.

But *First Things First*, let's talk about who needs these products. The estate planning "pros" are all in business to sell you their product. But just like the car dealer who will sell you a new car anytime you want one, it doesn't mean you really need it.

As we write this, anyone can leave roughly $5 million to any heir without any federal tax consequences. If your estate falls under that total value, a simple will is all you need. Just say where you want your money to go and make it legal. $100 if you do it yourself. $1000 with a good lawyer's help. That's it. Estate planned. Get on with life.

Our purpose here is to avoid the tax code minutia and the various exclusions, and how they all add up etc., so *Simplify.* We've rounded down and assume that $5 million will cover 99% of cases. But you probably don't need any help even at $6 million.

It gets better. The "portability" feature means a surviving spouse can use their own exemption plus the exemption of the previously deceased spouse. *There Will Be Math.* So now we're up to $10 million without any complicated advice being needed. (Be aware of this one, it's relatively new. In the dark ages, like 2007, trusts were used to bypass a spouse because the exemption was not transferable to them. "Portability" is a relatively new concept.)

So up to $10 million estate size, no problems. OK, let's please have a show of hands now. How many still need the rest of this chapter? We can't see you so we're not sure how many are left, but we're going to write on anyway because we're having fun. Hopefully, you are too.

First, to the truly wealthy who really do want to know more, we say congratulations. We'd all like to be in the top 1%, even though some of us will never admit it in public. Truly, well done!

We cannot do any hard-core estate planning here. There really are just too many things to consider specific to each individual circumstance. But we are going to discuss some universal concepts that should help everyone cut through the stupidity and get what they need.

It should be clear at this point that there are more people selling estate planning than there are customers who really need it. Stupid? Well, we keep saying there is a lot of stupidity out there. We just want to reduce it a little...

So how do you choose from among all the products and all the pros out there selling them to you?

First Things First. Here's the most important concept to accept. The government is going to get their taxes one way or another. The rules are always changing to keep up with avoidance strategies, the avoidance penalties are getting more severe, the audits are more targeted at the wealthy, and governments need more money every year. This all adds up to just accepting the inevitable, they will find a way to get their taxes.

Extreme efforts or expense may net you a little gain here or there. Yes, you really can hold gold in Singapore and probably avoid some taxes. But there's a good chance it will not be worth the effort. Or the risk.

Funny side story: US Eagles and South African Krugerrands are not pure enough to qualify as investment grade gold in Singapore. Stick with Canadian Maple Leafs or China's Gold Panda's if you go there. The USA and South African coins weigh a little more, and if smelted they do yield the stated percentage of gold, but the coins are alloys. Don't just weigh them and pay by the ounce.

Back to business. *Follow the Money*. Whatever extraordinary measures you take are very likely to be more profitable for someone else and just risky for you.

So the vast majority of worthwhile estate planning will have nothing to do with avoiding taxes. What you are really planning for is liquidity at your death. Your heirs will have to pay the taxes due. The very first thing you need to plan for is making sure your heirs aren't selling the estate to pay the taxes.

The traditional tool for liquidity at death is life insurance. *There Will Be Math*. This is a relatively simple proposal to consider. How much is your estimated estate tax, and how much does life insurance cost to cover that amount? Should you buy the insurance, or just set aside the cash? If you are married and using the portability feature, then you need a "second to die" policy. Added bonus for men, because women have longer life expectancy, you usually get better rates this way.

It's really no more complicated than that. Find a life insurance salesman you trust. (Is that an oxymoron or what?) OK seriously, if you have amassed net worth over $10 million, you must know an insurance salesman you trust by now. Right?

Find a life insurance salesman you trust and buy a term policy to cover the tax. Very roughly. If you're 70 years old, VERY ROUGHLY, expect to pay up to about $1000 per month for $1 million in coverage. Do we need to say VERY ROUGHLY again? We're just trying to give you an idea here. Hopefully, your trusted insurance agent comes in much lower. And don't forget the possible "second to die" savings.

Now, for the richest of the rich. If you want to set up a trust to take care of multiple generations of your descendants, then you do need a pro. The absolute best option is a trusted referral. If you have an attorney, ask them who they would recommend. Unless they are already a specialist, it should not offend them that you are asking for a referral rather than for them to do it themselves. This is a specialized field of study.

If you are really on your own and cannot find a referral to someone you trust, then we'd recommend finding one at the ACTEC. The American College of Trust and Estate Counsel. You will have to do some digging, but at least you are digging in the right place here.

We should also mention state taxes. As we write this there are about 15 states in the USA that collect estate or inheritance taxes in addition to the federal government. We cannot comment specifically on them, but you should be aware of their existence and know what's going on in your state. In general, they are considerably lower than the federal tax and your bigger concern should be to avoid overspending on planning that saves too little on taxes to be worth the effort. In general, if it means enough to you, relocate to a state that doesn't tax. That's the only safe way to avoid the tax.

Texas and Nevada are usually safe bets for avoiding "death taxes". But surprisingly, at the time we write this book, California does not have an estate tax either. How did they miss that one? Check it out. If you have net worth big enough to worry about it, chances are you can afford to establish residence in a state that doesn't tax inheritance.

In general, the best use of your estate planning time will be to support laws and politicians that reflect your idea of the correct tax, if any. There is considerable support for the idea of eliminating estate taxes altogether, but that is unlikely to happen anywhere when the government deficit is of greater concern.

The DontBeStupid.club Summary:

- The vast majority of people do not need complicated estate planning. They need a simple will.

- High net worth estates are going to pay taxes.

It's the society we live in.

- Keep it simple, and just plan for liquidity to help
your heirs with the taxes.

16.
Easy Answers

YOU PUT IN the effort to get here. Now we'll give you the easy answers we promised.

Define the Target. Easy - Achieved without great effort. Normally that is a recipe for failure when it comes to investing. This chapter is an exception to that rule.

OK, if you understand everything before this, then a good number of you are now thinking you really don't want to work that hard on your investments. And really, that is OK. Generally speaking, there is a correlation between frequent investing activity and failure. The sharks are just too good. And the more you swim around the more chances they will eat you.

Simplify. For most people, a "set it and forget it" approach works best. It has the added advantage of requiring the least amount of your effort. Very efficient.

But you have to set it up right in the first place. Being wrong at the beginning means it will stay wrong for a long time. And that would be stupid. So here are a couple of set-it-and-forget-it investments that are not stupid. Our hope is that you understand the concepts of investing well enough to know these are good, and well enough to ignore everyone who tries to take your money away from you under the disguise of helping you invest it. Now here are your easy answers.

Vanguard Target Date Retirement Funds. These mutual funds are a wonderfully simple choice. They have different target dates available. Know your goal, that means what year you plan to retire or start withdrawals, whichever is sooner. Buy the fund that most closely matches your date using your Vanguard investment account. Then whenever you have more money to invest, just buy more of your target date fund. That's it. You have professional managers buying a wide range of investments suitable for your goal. Your first choice is to buy it in your tax-deferred account, your 401k or IRA. If you hit the maximum deferral allowed by the government, then just open a taxable account and put the rest of your money in that way.

Our other easy answer is the **Vanguard Wellington Fund**. This is one of very few mutual funds that deserve discussion with religious reverence. If God exists in the world of investing, he's living in the Wellington Fund. This is a simple fund. Just very well-qualified people with high ethical standards running a mutual fund investing in high-quality stocks and bonds since 1929.

Through wars and depressions and panics, Wellington has been there for its investors. When you consider that about 95% of all mutual funds ever started don't even exist today, you get some idea of Wellington's stature within the industry. The smartest thing any competitor can do is just not mention it. To say something bad would just show their stupidity.

Wellington does not adjust their investment mix for your age and goal changes. To get that adjusting feature you would choose the target date retirement funds. But if the whole financial world was collapsing, you would want the Wellington fund managing your money.

If you can handle the complexity of two investments, it would be a formidable portfolio to split your money between a target date retirement fund and Wellington. There would be overlap in their holdings, but you would have two different styles managing your money. Wellington is selective while the target date funds do more on indexing.

Both styles achieve their goals while charging Vanguard's legendary low fees. The easiest answer is to buy one or the other. But buying both is still pretty easy and probably your best choice.

The DontBeStupid.club Summary:

- There are some easy answers that are also very good investments.

- The Vanguard Target Date Retirement funds and Vanguard Wellington fund are the best easy answers.

- This is a set it and forget it investment style. Ignore all the salespeople who try to change your course.

- Wellington has been reliably excellent since 1929. We like their chances in any disaster scenario.

- Owning both is easy and arguably a better portfolio than anyone could put together no matter how hard they work.

17.
Bonus Answer: Compounding

BELOW IS A chart you've seen many times before. This is the compounding chart everyone uses to sell their investing ideas. These charts are bullshit. Everything recurring compounds, it's not unique to any investment. *Don't Be Distracted*. And don't believe anyone who tells you Einstein said it was the greatest invention in history or anything like that. There is no evidence Mr. Einstein ever commented on the subject.

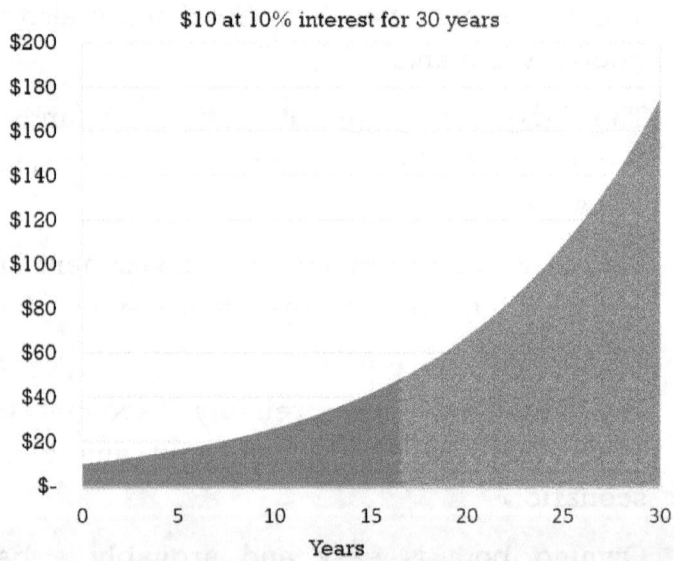

$10 at 10% interest for 30 years

The concept requires the (almost always flawed) assumption that a periodic gain remains constant over a large number of those time periods. As each period passes, you accumulate gains not only on your initial investment, but also on the accumulated gains since that initial investment. You get earnings on your earnings.

There Will Be Math. If you get 10% annual interest, then for a $10 investment you earn $1 of interest after one year. In the next year, you earn 10% on your $11 investment, so you get $1.10 of interest in year two. So now your invested total is up to $12.10, and you get $1.21 of interest in year 3. And so on and so on, increasing each year to infinity. Or more profoundly, compounding each year to infinity.

The fundamental problem with all sales pitches based on compounding assumptions is no investment returns are that constant. To put it another way, if our above example of $10 and 10% interest were true, then in only about 320 years we'd have all the money in the world. And still be compounding every year I guess... tough to sell us on that idea.

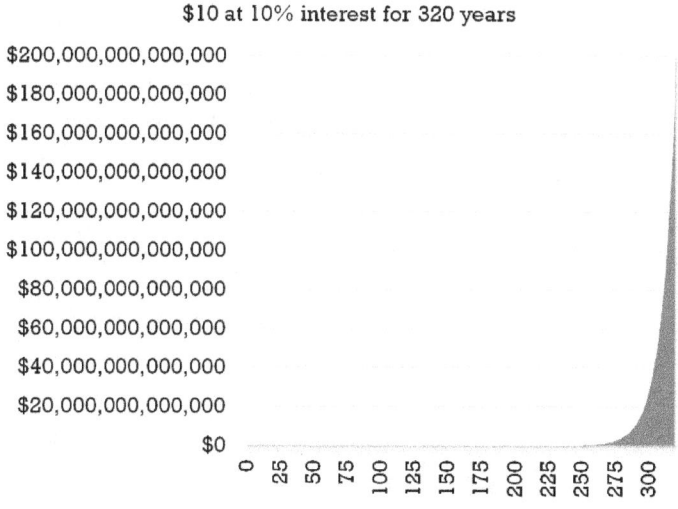

$10 at 10% interest for 320 years

The other problem, even more devious, is those dollars are not all created equal. Remember inflation? It devalues dollars and also compounds. To put it another way, if inflation matches your returns, then you gain nothing over the life of the compounding investment. Your dollars at the end buy the same thing as at the start. If someone shows you a chart with 8 or 10% compounded annual growth for 30 years, ask to see what investment actually delivered that return after inflation. Adjusted for inflation, the US stock market is actually negative since 2000. Compound that!

In real life, compounding actually should impact many of our decisions. In fact, it's something to consider frequently. Because there really is one way a return can be assured to remain constant for a known period of time, and that is if the event has already happened. The best use of the concept of compounding is to apply it to a decision you make today where the effect will be constant for a known period of time into the future.

For example, if you pay down a debt today, then you pay less interest on that debt for as long as it lasts. The return and the time period are known for certain. The value to you of that pay-down compounds over time.

Another nearly perfect use of the compounding concept is applying it to investing fees you do not pay. Fees are paid periodically and generally stated as an annual percent. Any expense you do NOT pay remains a part of your investment. It then compounds for whatever number of periods you continue with the investment. Compounding expenses is the single reason high expense investments have so little chance of outperformance over the long term.

As we go through life, compounding comes up all the time. Any decision made where the consequences repeat periodically is a candidate for compounding. Any time you consider monthly payments or adding interest expense to a purchase, you are compounding the cost. Ever see someone in great shape, maybe six-pack abs, chatting up the cutest girl on the beach? You're witnessing the compounding effect of some exercise.

Being aware of the compounding concept helps prioritize decisions. Things that are "one and done" just don't have the same importance as decisions where the effect compounds. If you are in a restaurant looking at the menu, how much you spend may have some compounding effect. If you buy wine that's so expensive you have to pay off the bill over several months, that is bad compounding. Maybe you should just have water instead. But whether you order the chicken sandwich or the hamburger probably doesn't matter too much.

The DontBeStupid.club Summary:

- When used in a chart to sell you something, compounding is usually just a distraction.

- But the compounding concept can be used in real life to make better decisions.

18.
Final Thoughts

WE'VE TRIED TO deliver a solid framework for preventing stupidity with investing.

We know we ruffled a lot of feathers, tread on some sacred cows, and messed with a lot of people's paychecks. Investing is big business. Investing stupidly supports a lot of jobs.

You know now that investing can take many different forms, but all can be simplified down to a few common elements. As soon as you leave these pages, you again will be barraged with information designed to make you think investing is terribly complicated, and that all those complicated products will make you rich. And you now recognize this is just an attempt by someone else to profit from your investments.

Don't Be Distracted. Remain clear in applying our principles and investing will always be simple.

There Will Be Math. You cannot escape the fact that investing requires math. In many cases, the math can be more complicated than the simple math usually required by our principle. But investing math is not something you have to do every day. You don't even do it every month if you're investing as we do. So when the time comes to do some math, you are ready to give it a little more effort than usual.

Most of all we hope you are much more aware of the constant sales pressure that pushes you toward stupid investing. And you are aware the universe of choices available to you is far broader than sales people would like you to think. Many of your best investments have no one selling them at all, you have to go looking for them.

And we hope you're a little bit angry about all the bullshit used to take your money away from you, all in the name of investing for your future. Maybe it will keep you sharp when the sharks start circling.

Investing is a very big topic. Billions of dollars are wasted on stupidity every year. We could write much more. We deliberately edited out topics we thought addressed too narrow an audience. Our goal here was just to deliver enough to make the world a little less stupid. If you'd like to see anything specific explored, please let us know. We'd love to help make the world even less stupid about money.

We've tried to keep it entertaining while informing on a subject where a lot of stupidity exists. We never intend to make light of an important subject. But Investing should never be so important that we cannot laugh about it. We've all made stupid investments. What else can you do but laugh about them? If you'd like to read about our stupidest move, see the bonus content on our website.

The more stupid we are, the more it costs us. Time, anxiety, cash, and frequently pain and suffering too. Stupidity is actually the BIGGEST business out there. They want us to be stupid. Everywhere we bleed money, someone hangs a bucket and collects.

We hope we made just a few dollars' difference here. Just a few dollars less stupidity for enough people, means we've succeeded in our mission to make the world a little less stupid.

Applying the DontBeStupid.club critical thought principles finds answers. Answers are the cure for stupidity. And, hopefully, now we are all a little less stupid about Investing.

19.
Don't Be Stupid Club

At DontBeStupid.club we make the world a little less stupid.

We do not take a position on an issue until we've thought about it critically. We always start with an *Open Mind*. We just apply our principles and think about the question. A little critical thinking is all that's required to quickly reach most answers. Sometimes a little more work is required. But we always get to the answer.

We don't care what people think. But we do care about how they think. Any well-reasoned opinion deserves respect. And opinions without basis are just stupid. Differing answers are fine. All we want is to make the world a little less stupid. If you hate our answer and have a well-reasoned opposition, GREAT!

We're all in this adventure together. We're stupid too. We are all conditioned from birth to think the wrong way. But we are a little less stupid for trying to fix that.

Critical thinking is a skill that can be learned. It's not even a difficult skill. It's harder to be a good welder or good coder or good baseball player. It's impossible for most of us to dunk a basketball. But we all can be good thinkers.

Critical thinking is a way of looking at the world. It's a

framework for thinking about anything. You're going to spend time thinking anyway, why not make the most of it? We think life is easier this way. You never feel lost if you know how to think.

Most disagreements we observe just come from people being stupid. Arguing points without defining their targets... adding complexity to hide their own inadequacies... trying to lie their way to a profit... going against nature... doing the wrong things first... all just stupid.

The world can be a much better place if we are all a little less stupid.

And know this. If you apply our critical thinking principles, then you can never be stupid. The stupidity is all around you, but it can never get YOU! Critical thinking is stronger than stupidity. Answers always equal power.

Our goal is to make a little difference in your life and entertain. Let us know how we did. We'd love to hear from you.

Visit http://DontBeStupid.club if you'd like more.

Our Amazon Store is located at: http://astore.amazon.com/dontbclub-20. It's where you'll find some of the products we like. Nothing in our store is stupid. You don't pay anything extra, but we get a little commission if you buy here. And we appreciate it. It helps us keep making the world a little less stupid.

We thank you for the time you spent with us.